OCS Report
MMS 2007-037

Investigation of Fatality and Loss of Well Control
High Island Block A466, Well No. B-11
OCS G-03242
20 February 2006

Gulf of Mexico
Off the Texas Coast

J. David Dykes – Chair
Richard Clingan
Jim Hail
Frank Patton

U.S. Department of the Interior
Minerals Management Service
Gulf of Mexico OCS Regional Office

New Orleans
June 2007

Contents

Executive Summary

An accident that resulted in one fatality and a brief loss of well control occurred on Forest Oil Corporation's (FOC) Platform B, High Island Block A-466, Well B-11, Lease OCS-G 03242 in the Gulf of Mexico, offshore the State of Texas, on February 20, 2006, at approximately 0820 hours. Forest Oil Corporation had hired the contractor, Twachtman, Snyder & Byrd, Incorporated (TSB), to conduct plug and abandonment operations on Well B-11.

From February 14, 2006, to February 19, 2006, plug and abandonment operations were being conducted on the subject well. The tubing was being stripped out of the hole by using a hydraulic rig (casing jacks) when the tubing became stuck on February 19, 2006. On the morning of February 20, 2006, an attempt was made by FOC's "company man" to pull the tubing, when the tubing parted. The parted tubing was forced upward, causing the top slips to be ejected from the top bowl of the casing jacks. The ejected slips fatally struck FOC's "company man" as he attempted to evacuate the immediate area.

This investigative panel has concluded, based on information in the report findings, that the deceased exceeded the yield strength of the tubing when he pulled approximately 135,000 pounds on the tubing, causing it to part. This resulted in the tubing and slips being ejected from the wellbore, the slips fatally striking the deceased as he attempted to evacuate the area, and a brief loss of well control. It is also the conclusion of this panel that the deceased did not calculate enough of a safety factor when he determined maximum amount pull for the grade of pipe. Furthermore, this panel concludes that the lack of appropriate equipment (snubbing unit) and appropriately trained personnel are contributing causes to this incident. Additionally, poor judgment and decisionmaking by the deceased and TSB's field supervisors on the platform are also considered contributing causes to this incident. This investigative panel has also concluded that ineffective management and supervision of the operation by both FOC and TSB (at all levels) is a possible contributing cause of this incident. Upper management at FOC and TSB were detached from the field operation and failed to provide direct oversight and control. At TSB, no effective chain of command structure was in place and no one in the office was overseeing the operation. FOC relied entirely on consultants to supervise the operation onsite and offsite. The deceased exceeded his authority and made operational decisions on behalf of FOC and TSB without input from management.

Introduction

Authority

An accident that resulted in one fatality and a brief loss of well control occurred on Forest Oil Corporation's (FOC) Platform B, High Island Block A-466, Lease OCS-G 03242 in the Gulf of Mexico, offshore the State of Texas, on February 20, 2006, at approximately 0820 hours. Pursuant to 43 U.S.C. 1348(d)(1) and (2) and (f) [Outer Continental Shelf (OCS) Lands Act, as amended] and Department of the Interior regulations 30 CFR 250, the Minerals Management Service (MMS) is required to investigate and prepare a public report of this accident. By memorandum dated February 23, 2006, the following personnel were named to the investigative panel:

> J. David Dykes, Chairman – Office of Safety Management, GOM OCS Region;
>
> James Hail – Lake Jackson District, Field Operations, GOM OCS Region;
>
> Frank Patton – New Orleans District, Field Operations, GOM OCS Region;
>
> Richard Clingan – Accident Investigation Board, Office of Offshore Regulatory Programs,
> Offshore Minerals Management

The panel members met numerous times throughout the investigation to conduct interviews, review the facts of the incident, draw necessary conclusions, and prepare this report.

Background

Lease OCS-G 03242 covers approximately 5,760 acres and is located in High Island Block A-466, Gulf of Mexico, off the Texas Coast. (*For lease location, see Attachment 1.*) The lease was issued to Atlantic Richfield Company, effective September 1, 1975. Forest Oil Corporation became owner and designated operator of the lease on December 7, 2000, and was the operator of record at the time of the incident. Mariner Energy, through a merger/acquisition, has become the designated operator of the lease.

Findings

Physical Living Conditions Onsite

This job was taking place on platform "B" in High Island Block A466. "B" platform is an eight-pile structure with a top deck and a cellar deck. The top and cellar decks have an approximate dimension of 130 ft by 60 ft. (*See Attachment 2 for Photograph of Platform.*)

This is an unmanned facility that has been targeted to be plugged and abandoned. The platform is equipped with a 10-feet by 20-feet emergency quarters/office building designed only to provide shelter in inclement weather. According to the TSB personnel interviewed, the TSB crew would use a portable 6-man sleeper/office and the quarters available on the field boat (*M/V Lytal Queen*). The only bathroom facilities were the use of a port-o-let (porta-potty) on the platform and the bathroom facilities on the boat. Meals were prepared on the boat by the crew of the M/V *Lytal Queen*. Lifesaving equipment consisted of two life-floats and eight life ring buoys. There is an escape capsule on the platform; however, it out of service.

Preliminary Activities - Plug and Abandonment Procedures

The regulations at 30 CFR 250.613(b) require in part that the following information be submitted with MMS Form 124:

- A brief description of the well workover procedures to be followed, a statement of the expected surface pressure, and type and weight of workover fluids;
- When changes in existing subsurface equipment are proposed, a schematic drawing of the well showing the zone proposed for workover and the workover equipment to be used;

On May 5, 2005, Forest Oil contracted Tetra Technologies to conduct a turnkey abandonment of 11 wells on HI A466 Platform B. The original procedure to abandon this well was submitted to MMS Lake Jackson District Office on July 11 and approved July 12, 2005. This procedure was a standard procedure, but did not indicate the type of equipment that would be used to accomplish the abandonment. The procedure only mentioned pumps and wireline operations. On October 10, 2005, verbal approval was granted to Forest Oil allowing a coil tubing unit to remove obstructions on wells B-8, B-10, and B-11. Tetra began work on B-11 on October 19, 2005, using coil tubing equipment, but shut down the

3

operation on October 21, 2005, after several unsuccessful attempts at retrieving the subsurface safety valve (storm choke). Tetra rigged down their equipment and secured the well with approximately 1,000 psi on the casing and the storm choke stuck in the landing nipple at 629 feet measured depth.

A revised procedure was submitted and approved on December 8, 2005, for the use of a snubbing unit with additional pumping equipment. The procedure did not indicate that there would be a pressure problem. It stated they would fill the casing and tubing with fluid. Just prior to the beginning of operations, another revised permit was submitted on February 9 and approved on February 14, 2006, to use casing jacks. The revised procedure submitted to MMS was the same procedure previously submitted and approved by MMS, with casing jacks substituted for snubbing equipment. FOC contracted TSB to complete the plug and abandonment of the B11 well.

When operations began on February 14, 2006, the shut-in tubing pressure was 1,900 psi, which was bled to zero. The shut-in casing pressure was 700 psi, which could not be bled to zero. A plug was set in the tubing with a slickline unit at 300 feet wireline measurements, and the blowout preventers (BOP) were set up. The installation of the BOP's and testing continued on the 15th and 16th, and the operations began on the 16th, when TSB released the packer on the tubing string. Four barrels of weighted fluid were pumped down the casing to fill the hole prior to releasing the packer.

In an e-mail dated February 14, 2006, from the deceased to the president of TSB, the deceased discussed killing the subject well with seawater. The e-mail reads as follows:

> The tubing had a SITP of 1900 psi. The tubing will bleed to 0 psi within 20 seconds of opening the choke. The production casing had a shut-in pressure of 700 psi. We are presently testing the intermediate casing. We will N/U BOPs afterwards. I will contact you and D.J. when we have a better idea of the timing for pulling the packer free. We intend to use the production casing as a means to pump into the well or to keep the hole full while pulling tubing. A column of seawater from the surface to the packer has a hydrostatic equivalent of 4242 psi the tubing builds up to 1900 psi with 0 fluids when bleeding down. The column of fluid in the casing will have a greater hydrostatic pressure than the well. This will allow you to have sufficient fluid to kill/control the well once the packer is released and the fluid can reach the perforations.

Operations began on the 17th to start pulling tubing from the well by using the casing jacks. The operation involved stripping the tubing through the annular preventer. Stripping pipe through the annular preventer is a critical operation because this task can damage the annular element. Eight joints of tubing were removed. The well began flowing ¼ barrel per minute of 8.6-ppg fluid and the crew initiated "lube and bleed" operations to try to control the flow. TSB crewmembers stated during the interviews that they would just fill the hole and bleed it off. The crew continued having trouble controlling the pressure on the well and only one additional joint of tubing was removed prior to the accident.

According to the TSB crewmembers, the lubrication and bleed procedures consisted of the following:

- Pump seawater into the casing.

- Wait anywhere from 5 to 60 minutes for fluid to fall.

- Bleed off gas pressure either through the gas buster or directly at the choke/kill spool at tree.

According to the TSB daily report dated February 18, 2006, the crew pumped 42 bbls of seawater into the casing from 0001 hours to 0200 hours. Pressure rose to 3,000. They monitored for 15 minutes, then bled off the pressure and got back 39 bbls of fluid. From 0200 hours to 0400 hours, they pumped 40 bbls of seawater and monitored for 15 minutes. From 0400 hours to 0600 hours, the pumped an additional 30 bbls of seawater and monitored for 15 minutes. At 1300 hours, they pumped 100 bbls for three hours. From 1600 to 1800 hours, they attempted to bleed pressure off the casing and got back 75 bbls of fluid.

The industry-accepted practice of lubricating and bleeding operations includes the following key points:

- Determine pressure on casing, including hydrostatic pressure of the formation.

- Determine hydrostatic equivalent for volume of fluid to be pumped.

- Pump fluid into the wellbore or annulus and allow it to fall.

- Allow sufficient time (at least a half hour) for the well to stabilize.

- Bleed off pressure of gas equivalent to the hydrostatic pressure of the volume of fluid pumped.

Activity Subsequent to the Incident

After the accident, a procedure for using a snubbing unit was submitted, and the operation was successfully completed. This operation included removing the equipment stuck in the hole, circulating a proper density kill fluid, setting cement plugs, and removing the tubing from the wellbore. The initial procedure to use a snubbing unit, approved in December, did not address the storm choke stuck in the tubing, but could have effectively handled this problem. Using the casing jacks, TSB was trying to get the tubing out of the hole to the obstruction; hot tap the tubing below the obstruction, equalizing the pressure and fluid level in the tubing and casing annulus; and then proceeding with the plugging operations. The use of casing jacks presupposes that the well is dead.

Incidents of Noncompliance Issued

On March 2, 2006, the MMS Lake Jackson District Manager requested a meeting with Forest Oil Company to discuss the fatality at HI A466 'B' and the safety and planning for the latest proposed plug and abandonment (P&A) procedures, schedules, service companies and the equipment to be used. Representing Forest Oil were the Gulf Coast Region Manager; the Project Manager for HI A466 B-11 P&A; the Assistant General Counsel; the Vice-President of Shelf and Offshore; and the Environmental, Health, and Safety Manager.

During the meeting on March 2, 2006, MMS issued four Incidents of Noncompliance (INC) to Forest Oil and they are listed below:

- G-112 C Lessee does not provide for the safety of all personnel and take necessary precautions to correct and remove any Hazardous Oil and Gas accumulation or other health, safety, or fire hazards (RE: Grating missing from casing jack at the well slot B-11, bolts missing from casing jack riser joints).

- Z-135 C At the BOP's and well tree, the deck does not have suitable guards or handrails.

- W-122 C No remote control station in a readily accessible location.

- W-120 C No automatic backup accumulator charging system with a power source independent from the power source of the primary accumulator charging system.

MMS issued four additional INC's to the operator on March 3, 2006, and forwarded those to the operator by mail. Those INC's were as follows:

- W-162 W   All records, including pressure charts, operations logs, and reference documents of BOP tests, actuations, and inspections, were removed from the facility.

- G-116 C   Operations were not conducted in accordance with approved plans (RE: rigging down and removal of casing jack).

- W-115 C   MMS's approval of 2 pipe rams, 1 blind ram, 1 annular; (Lessee only installed 1 pipe ram, 1 blind ram, and 1 annular)

- W-153 C   The Well #B-11 was not equipped with a pump-through type tubing plug and a back-pressure valve prior to removal of the tree.

Blowout Prevention Equipment Information

The approved permit displayed a drawing of the blowout preventer (BOP) stack to be used. The diagram shows a 7 1/16 inch, 5000-pound BOP with 1 annular, 2 pipe rams, 1 blind ram, and a spool with a proper choke kill valve configuration. *(See Attachment 3 for diagram of approved BOP configuration.)* Observations made following the incident indicate that the BOP stack was not configured as approved. The configuration of the BOP stack consisted of 1 annular, 1 pipe ram, 1 blind ram, and a choke/kill Spool. The choke/kill spool consisted of 1 manual valve for the choke line and 1 manual valve for the kill line. *(See Attachment 4 of picture of BOP stack on location.)*

According to the approved procedures dated February 14, 2006, the BOP's were to be tested by using sea water to 250 pounds for the low and 5,000 pounds for the high. The TSB morning report of February 16, 2006, states that the BOP's were tested from 11:30 to 12:30 with 250 pounds for the low and 3,000 pounds for the high. Each was tested for 15 minutes apiece. The total test time was one hour. According to the TSB day-crew supervisor's tally book, on the fifth page it was recorded, "nipple up BOPs from 11:30 – 12:30 and test from 12:30 – 15:30." This indicates a total test time of three hours.

The regulations at 30 CFR 250.615(c) state in part that the BOP systems for well workover operations with the tree removed shall be equipped with......a choke line and a kill line each equipped with two full opening valves and a choke manifold. At least one of the valves on the choke-line shall be remotely controlled. At least one of the valves on the kill line shall be remotely controlled, except that a check valve on the kill line in lieu of the remotely controlled valve may be installed, provided two readily accessible manual valves are in place and the check valve is placed between the manual valves and the pump. *(See Attachment 4 of picture of BOP stack on location.)*

The regulations at 30 CFR 250.616(a), "Blowout preventer systems testing, records, and drills," state that prior to the conducting of high-pressure tests, all BOP system components shall be successfully tested to a low pressure of 200 to 300 psi. Ram-type BOP's, related control equipment, including the choke and kill manifolds, and safety valves shall be successfully tested to the rated working pressure of the BOP equipment or as otherwise approved by the District Manager.

The regulations at 30 CFR 250.616(d) state that the lessee shall record pressure conditions during BOP tests on pressure charts, unless otherwise approved by the District Manager. The test interval for each BOP component tested shall be sufficient to demonstrate that the component is effectively holding pressure. The charts shall be certified as correct by the operator's representative at the facility.

The regulations at 30 CFR 250.616(e) state that the time, date, and results of all pressure tests, actuations, inspections.....shall be recorded in the operations log. The BOP tests shall be documented in accordance with the following: (1) The documentation shall indicate the sequential order of BOP and auxiliary equipment testing and the pressure and duration of each test.

Neither Forest Oil nor TSB have provided a BOP test chart as proof of the BOP having been tested. In all of the records supplied to the investigation, there is no record of other BOP components and/or valves being listed as tested.

Tubing Specifications

The High Island Block A-466 Well B11 was originally drilled and completed in 1989. There have been no sidetracks, bypasses, or re-completions on this well; therefore, the tubing in the well is approximately 17 years old. It is not known whether or not this tubing had been used in an earlier well completion. The tubing string identified in the plug and abandonment procedures, submitted to MMS on December 8, 2005, had the following specifications:

8

O.D (inch)	Weight (lb/ft)	Grade	Connection	Set Depth
2 7/8"	6.5	L80	EUE	9590'

According to the *Halliburton Cementing Tables Handbook*, the *Western Engineers Handbook*, and the *Association of Energy Service Companies Basic Data Manual*, this tubing has a joint yield strength of 145,000 pounds.

During the interviews, the TSB day-crew supervisor stated that he recalled that the TSB job supervisor (the deceased) informed him that the breaking strength of the tubing was approximately 140,000 pounds and that the maximum pull should not exceed 120-130,000 pounds (approximately 80-90% of the actual joint yield strength of 145,000 pounds).

The daily morning reports do not disclose the maximum allowable pull weight for the tubing string; however, it is noted on the report dated February 16, 2006, that the tubing was worked from 68,000 to 98,000 pounds until the packer released. It is also noted on the daily report dated, February 19, 2006, that 130,000 pounds were pulled on the tubing in attempting to free the stuck tubing. Furthermore, the TSB night-crew wireline operator stated during the interview that he was operating the casing jacks when the 130,000 pounds were pulled. He indicated that he left the pipe in tension with 113,000 pounds on the tubing. He further stated that he showed the TSB job supervisor (the deceased) where the pipe had stretched.

Post-incident evaluation/analysis of the hydraulic power pump was conducted by FOC and Deepwell Rentals at the Deepwell Rentals Houma facility. Upon receiving the pump at Deepwell, the relief valve for the hydraulic power pump was tested and the set point was found to be 1,200 psi. This set point indicates a pulling capacity of 135,720 pounds.

FOC obtained the services of Exponent Failure Analysis Associates (EFAA) to conduct an examination of the parted tubing sections to determine if any deficiency in the tubing caused or contributed to the parting of the tubing joint. FOC advised EFAA that destructive testing of the parted tubing sections should not be undertaken; however, FOC did provide EFAA with an additional joint of identical tubing from the same tubing string from the subject well. The following is taken in part from EFAA's analysis summary report:

"......The tubing of both the accident and exemplar was measured to be 2.91 inches diameter, with a wall thickness of 0.25 inches. The intact exemplar section of tubing was 32 feet 9 inches long. The accident tubing was in two sections, and had been stretched as a result of the applied forces, so its original length could only be estimated to be approximately the same as the exemplar tubing section. Based on the results of the testing described below, I determined that the tubing was produced to API Specification 5A, Grade N-80.

The exemplar section of tubing was destructively tested to the requirements of API Specification 5A, Grade N-80 (March 1982) by machining the specified tensile samples and pulling them to failure. The exemplar tubing was found to meet all of the tensile requirements (yield strength, tensile strength, and elongation) of the 5A, Grade N-80 specification. Hardness testing was also performed on five sections of the exemplar tubing for comparison to hardness testing that was performed on the accident section of pipe. Within the experimental error inherent in hardness testing of intact tubing with a portable hardness tester, the accident tubing was found to meet the tensile requirements of API Specification 5A with an estimated tensile yield stress of approximately 85,000 psi (pounds per square inch).

Further, the fracture region of the subject pipe was examined optically and by measurements. Significant ductile elongation and reduction of area was observed at the fracture site, confirming that the tubing was sufficiently ductile and free of metallurgical or geometric stress risers. The absence of anomalies on the fracture surface is further evidence that the accident tubing was free of defects.

To compare the strength of this tubing to the specifications published in the *Halliburton Cementing Tables Handbook* ....it is necessary to convert the intrinsic yield stress of the tubing, in pounds per square inch, into the strength of the tubing, expressed in pounds. The area of the tubing, in square inches, can be computed from the formula for the area of a hollow circle

10

$$\text{Area} = \pi/4(D^2\text{-}d^2)$$

where D is the outer diameter of the tubing and d is the inner diameter of the tubing.

For 2.875 inch tubing with a 2.441 inch inner diameter, the area of the tubing is 1.812 square inches. Multiplying this area by the minimum yield stress of the tubing, 80,000 pounds per square inch, yields an overall strength of 144,960 pounds, which is exactly the value found in the *Halliburton Cementing Tables Handbook* for 2.875 inch tubing joint yield strength for an upset threaded and coupled joint of N-80 tubing.

Following this analytical technique, the panel applied the same formula, and using the actual tensile yield of 85,000 pounds per square inch (determined from the destructive testing by EFAA), calculated that the yield on the subject pipe was approximately 154,020 pounds. EFAA described the destructive test method during a follow-up interview and indicated that the environmental conditions (age, corrosion, internal/external pressure, etc.,) of the subject pipe could have reduced the actual yield of the subject pipe by approximately 15-20 percent. This reduction indicates a calculated potential yield range of 123,216 pounds to 130,917 pounds.

Job Safety Analyses

Numerous job safety analyses (JSA) were created during this plug and abandonment job. The panel reviewed approximately 32 JSA's that were used over the course of seven days. These JSA's covered the following eleven topics:

Rig Up and Pull Tubing with Casing Jacks	Bullhead Down Tubing	Crane Operations
Rig Up Plug & Abandonment Equipment	Boat Work	Police Deck
Nipple Up Blowout Prevention Stack	Mixing Cement	Cutting With Torch
Break Out Tubing	Pumping Operations	

A review of the JSA's by panel members revealed the following:

- The JSA's are generated on the computer by the TSB crew supervisors. Areas covered in the JSA's include Protective Equipment Required or Recommended, Safety Measures Required or Recommended, Required Appropriate Work Permits, Personnel Required to Perform This Job, List Specialized Equipment Required by Job Scope, and List Basic Steps Required for Safe Completion of Job. There is no reference in the JSA's to specific pieces of equipment for which the hazards need to be avoided.

- Most of the JSA's are generic in content. Very few are specific with respect to what equipment is to be used and/or specific steps for setting up the equipment. Most of the hazards that are identified are the generic slip, trip, and falls; pinch points; hearing hazards; etc. No hazards were identified for the specific operation.

- All of the JSA's identify the number of personnel required for the job tasks; however, according to a tally of the signatures of the participants, most of the JSA's did not have enough participants to conduct the jobs.

- Hot work was conducted on February 14, 2006. According to the hot work permit, the flowline flange was cut away. Hot work was again conducted on February 16, 2006. According to this hot work permit, the grating around the well-head was removed. Neither of these specific jobs included a JSA for the work to be conducted.

- During the interviews, some of the TSB crewmembers stated that JSA's were discussed and reviewed during every pre-job safety meeting prior to starting their tour, while other TSB crewmembers indicated that the JSA's were not discussed or reviewed and safety meetings were not conducted. These crewmembers indicated that they were instructed to sign the JSA's prior to beginning work.

- There was no JSA created for the "lubrication and bleeding" of fluid into the production annulus of the well to kill the well.

- There was no JSA created for taking returns to the gas buster following the "lubrication and bleeding" process.

- TSB had a JSA for Rigging Up & Pulling Pipe with Casing Jacks. This JSA did not specifically address stripping pipe under pressure with the casing jacks.

Observed and Documented Unsafe Acts

During the interviews, several TSB crewmembers expressed their concern about the use of casing jacks. The day-crew electric line operator stated that casing jacks are not considered normal for this type of job. The day-crew wireline operator also stated "nothing about this job was normal." He further stated that he voiced his concern to the deceased and that he [the deceased] appeared to be in another world. The night-crew senior pump operator stated that he questioned the deceased at the dock about not using a snubbing unit. He stated that the deceased told him that the decision was his [the deceased].

TSB crewmembers stated that the annular control lines were reversed. Further, several crewmembers stated that the remote BOP control station was either not hooked up or did not function, while other crewmembers stated that the remote station was hooked up and did function. Further testimony indicated that the remote station shared the same air supply line as the crane. According to the TSB crewmembers onsite at the time of the incident, they shut in the BOP from the accumulator unit located on the well/production deck and not from the remote BOP station (located on the main/top deck).

During a review of pictures taken by a TSB crewmember, another TSB crewmember was observed operating the choke on the gas buster. The choke is located on top of the trip tank at an elevation greater than six feet off the deck and near the outside edge of the platform *(See Attachment 5 of photograph of TSB crewmember working without fall protection)*. TSB's *Supervisor's Health/Safety/Environmental Manual and Training Guide* (Safety Manual) states in the section titled "Personal Protective Equipment Programs," subsection "Fall Protection," the following:

> Safety harnesses.....are mandatory when working above the ground. This equipment must be worn and tied off to independent life lines, overhead pipe or structures when working from elevated areas under the following conditions:
> - Working six feet above ground elevation or platform
> - Two-point suspension scaffolds or stages are in use

- Working off scaffolds
- Ladders are placed near the edge of a roof or floor opening
- Elevated work where no protection is available to prevent the worker from falling requires 100 percent tie-off at all times.

TSB's safety manual further states that the personal protective equipment training will be documented by identifying the employees trained, date of training, and instructor. The training documentation is kept on file for each employee. A review of the TSB crewmembers' training records provided to this investigative panel indicates that none had received any personal protective equipment training.

During the interviews, several TSB crewmembers stated that they had observed unsafe acts by the supervisory personnel. One crewmember stated that he observed the deceased in the work area without safety toe shoes and hard hat.

Another crewmember stated that he observed the TSB day crew supervisor bleeding the gas off the casing at the wellhead instead of bleeding it off through the gas buster *(see Attachment 6 for photograph of bleeding gas at BOP stack)*. The result of the action led to pollution of the Gulf waters *(see Attachment 7 for photograph of pollution)*.

When the TSB day crew supervisor was shown photographs of the lube and bleed procedure (blowing down the well overboard through the choke and kill lines) during the interview, he conceded that it must have made a sheen and "[he] shouldn't have done it."

The regulations at 30 CFR 250.300 state that during the exploration, development, production, and transportation of oil and gas or sulphur, the lessee shall take measures to prevent unauthorized discharge of pollutants into the offshore waters. The lessee shall not create conditions that will pose unreasonable risk to public health, life, property, aquatic life, wildlife, recreation, navigation, commercial fishing, or other uses of the ocean.

According to the TSB crewmembers, on Sunday, February 19, 2006, the M/V *Lytal Queen* was being sent in to the dock to take the senior pump operator in for a back injury that he had experienced earlier in the week. The deceased informed the night crew staying on the boat that they would have to stay/sleep "hot

14

sheet" on the platform while the boat went to the dock. Several crewmembers expressed their concern to the deceased about "hot sheeting" and overall safety on the facility and refused to stay on the facility. According to their statements, the deceased informed them that if they went in to the dock, they would be fired.

Project Management

Forest Oil Company (FOC) operated HIA-466 Platform B at the time of the incident. FOC's linear reporting structure for Gulf Coast Region operations is illustrated in *Attachment 8*. The principal individuals managing the B-11 well abandonment on February 20, 2006, for FOC were the

- Vice President of Operations, Gulf Coast Region (Operations VP);
- Operations Manager, Gulf Coast Region;
- Private consultant in charge of managing the day-to-day operation in the office (offsite) (FOC office consultant); and the
- TSB consultant/FOC "company man" on the platform (the deceased).

Twachtman, Snyder, & Byrd, Inc. (TSB) was the primary contractor conducting the B-11 well abandonment for FOC. TSB's reporting structure for "normal" plug and abandonment (P&A) operations, and for the subject operation, is indicated in *Attachments 9 & 10*, respectively. The individuals involved in the operation were

- TSB President in charge of decommissioning and P&A operations
- TSB Downhole Division Operations Manager
- Sales representative with the sales group
- TSB consultant/FOC "company man" on the platform (the deceased)
- Field supervisors with the Downhole Division.

Forest Oil Corporation Management Responsibilities

The responsibilities and actions of FOC's project management team prior to and immediately following the incident are detailed below. In conjunction with this investigation, we interviewed the Operations Manager for the Gulf Coast Region and FOC's office consultant. We declined to interview the Vice-President of Operations for the Gulf Coast Region. During the interviews, the FOC Operations Manager

15

stated that he reported to the Vice-President of Operations and spoke daily with FOC's Vice-President of Operations for the Gulf Coast Region; however, those conversations did not routinely include specifics of the subject operation.

Operations Manager

During the interview, the Operations Manager stated that on May 5, 2005, he contracted Tetra Technologies to plug and abandon the B-11 well by using coil tubing, as previously discussed. Tetra was unsuccessful in completing the operation and the Operations Manager subsequently assigned FOC's office consultant to complete the abandonment. He also stated that during the planning phase that he

- drafted the initial snubbing procedure and approved the final snubbing procedure prior to submittal to MMS;

- approved the revised procedure and equipment change from a snubbing unit to casing jacks prior to submittal to MMS because it would save time and money and because he assumed the well could be easily killed;

- tasked FOC's office consultant with locating an additional consultant to oversee the onsite operation; and

- requested a copy of the deceased's lubricate and bleed procedure, which he never received.

When shown the photographs of the lube and bleed process (blowing down gas through the choke and kill lines and causing pollution), the Operations Manager stated that he was unaware that TSB had been blowing down gas through the choke and kill lines. He stated that he would have shut down the operation if he had known about the lube and bleed procedure and resulting pollution.

During the conduct of the operation, the FOC Operations Manager briefed the FOC Operations VP on the progress of the operation, based on information submitted by the deceased in the morning reports and passed on to him by the FOC office consultant. The FOC Operations Manager was on personal time from February 17-20, 2006. He told the panel members that he was concerned about the length of time it was taking to kill the well and complete the job. He further indicated that he intended to address those concerns when he returned to work on Tuesday, February 21, if the situation remained unchanged.

The morning reports revealed that TSB was having problems killing the well, but did not indicate the occurrence of unsafe work practices or pollution on the platform, or that several crew members had left the platform because they felt the job was unsafe.

FOC Office Consultant

The FOC Office Consultant is a petroleum engineer and private consultant specializing in drilling, workover, and abandonment operations. He was hired by FOC (Denver) to supervise several drilling projects in the Gulf Coast Region and was assigned the task of abandoning the subject well on December 5, 2005, by the FOC Operations Manager.

The FOC Office Consultant stated in the interviews that during the planning phase, he did the following:

- Reviewed Tetra's previous coil tubing work on B-11 and was aware of the pressure consideration, but felt the pressure would be dealt with in time and that the well would be killed. He would have preferred conducting another coil tubing operation; however, the FOC Operations Manager rejected the idea, as it had been tried before and had failed.

- Hired the deceased to manage the project onsite with the expressed understanding that the deceased would maintain a "wall" between himself and the TSB crews conducting the operation (which would have precluded him from operating the equipment) and "take no chances."

- Revised the original snubbing procedure to substitute casing jacks for the snubbing equipment (as previously discussed).

- Submitted the revised procedure to MMS for approval.

- Contracted TSB to plug and abandon the well.

- Reviewed the original snubbing procedure with the deceased and the TSB day-crew supervisor) prior to mobilizing the operation.

FOC initially selected a snubbing company as the primary contractor for the snubbing work, with TSB providing supporting e-line, wireline, pumping, and consulting services. Following several site visits to the facility, the deceased recommended the equipment substitution referenced in the revised procedure for the reasons cited below. At the invitation of the TSB sales group, the FOC office consultant met with the deceased and the TSB sales representative and discussed the B-11 well abandonment.

The FOC Office Consultant approved the deceased's recommendation to substitute casing jacks for snubbing equipment because of the following considerations:

- He considered the use of casing jacks to be normal for this type of operation (a consideration based on his previous experience).

- He had used casing jacks once before on a "live well."

- He assumed the well could be killed with seawater once the packer was unseated (an assumption based on his previous experience).

- He assumed the tubing string would remain "pipe heavy" throughout the operation (an assumption based on his previous experience).

- Industry-wide Post-Katrina deficiencies in experienced personnel and equipment limited his options in selecting contractors and vessels.

- He was unable to locate suitable portable housing or a vessel to accommodate all personnel needed for both snubbing and wire line operations and, therefore, he needed to reduce the number of contract personnel by half in order to house everyone on the platform and vessel.

- The deceased (and possibly the TSB sales representative) indicated that TSB had experienced personnel available to do the job with casing jacks and that he (the deceased) didn't need a second crew (snubbing crew) to P&A the well.

- He could reduce project costs by reducing the number of contract personnel and equipment on the job.

The FOC Office Consultant made the decision to contract the abandonment work to TSB for the reasons cited above. In addition, FOC had an existing Master Service Agreement (MSA) for time and materials with TSB, which simplified the process.

The FOC Office Consultant stated that, during the conduct of the operation, he reviewed the morning reports submitted by the deceased each day and discussed the progress with the FOC Operations Manager. The FOC Office Consultant typically had telephone conversations in the morning with the deceased and at other times as needed; the conversations were mainly goal oriented and not detailed. The deceased never revealed either in conversation or in the morning reports that any improper or unsafe work practices or pollution had occurred during the operation, only that TSB was having difficulty killing the well. The FOC Office Consultant was not concerned by this situation and believed that the well would be killed in time, based on his experience.

On the two days prior to the day of the accident (February 18 and 19), the FOC Office Consultant spoke with the deceased on three separate occasions. During those conversations, the deceased never provided the FOC Office Consultant with a complete and accurate picture of the conduct and progress of the operation, the difficulties encountered, or any indication that the job wasn't headed in the right direction. The FOC Office Consultant didn't learn that TSB had been pulling forcefully on the pipe until he read about it in the morning report on February 20 (for activities conducted on February 19), which the deceased transmitted approximately 45 minutes before the incident.

The FOC Office Consultant visited the platform in December 2005 and never revisited the platform (or witnessed the operation) until February 21, 2006, following the accident. At that time, he accompanied the United States Coast Guard (USCG) to the platform, where the USCG conducted a site investigation and interviewed several contract personnel. According to the FOC Office Consultant, prior to February 21, 2006, he was unaware of

- equipment malfunctions (BOP) other than a minor problem with the crane;

- the deceased's practice of operating the casing jacks;

- unsafe work practices and safety concerns of the crew;

- the deceased's lubricate and bleed procedure and the resulting pollution;

- the crew working through the night despite being shorthanded after six crew members left the job;

- the deceased's gag order preventing the crew from communicating with managers offsite and with the TSB Downhole Division Manager in particular;

- the deceased's lack of communication or coordination with anyone onshore at TSB;

- TSB's poor housekeeping practices; and

- the force applied to the pipe in attempting to free the tubing.

Twachtman, Snyder & Byrd, Inc. Management Responsibilities

The responsibilities and actions of TSB's managers and field supervisors prior to and immediately following the incident are detailed below. In conjunction with this investigation, we interviewed the TSB President in charge of decommissioning and P&A operations and the TSB Downhole Division Manager. We also interviewed the TSB day and night crew supervisors on the platform. We declined to interview the TSB sales representative as his involvement in this incident appears to have been limited to the acquisition of the contract rather than the onsite or offsite management of the operation.

The TSB President

The TSB President is a professional engineer and partner in charge of decommissioning and P&A operations. He was also the supervisor of the deceased. The TSB President stated that he considered the subject operation to be "unusual" for TSB, but he never perceived the job to be unsafe or one the company was ill-equipped to handle.

The TSB President was not in favor of the deceased working in the field and would have preferred keeping him in the office where he could work on multiple projects. He felt that FOC needed the deceased's expertise onsite and reluctantly agreed to the arrangement.

Beyond approving the deceased's consulting assignment with FOC, the TSB president did not manage or oversee any of the work. The TSB president left the coordination and consultation up to the deceased and the TSB Downhole Division Manager. He expected that

- the TSB Downhole Division Manager would initially coordinate crews and equipment mobilized for the job, obtain daily reports from the platform, consult with the deceased as needed, and generally stay abreast of progress and problems with the operation day-to-day, and

- the deceased would be working for FOC as a consultant on the platform and function as TSB's primary contact with FOC on the job.

During the interview, the TSB President stated that he understood that the decision to substitute casing jacks for the snubbing equipment was FOC's decision. He was surprised to learn that the deceased had not consulted with the TSB Downhole Division Manager during the operation and that there was discord and disagreement between the two men from the beginning, regarding the conduct and oversight of the operation. According to the TSB President, the TSB Downhole Division Manager called him daily but did not mention these kinds of problems in any of their conversations. The TSB President apparently never had a clear understanding of FOC's intention to use the deceased as their "company man" on the platform nor envisioned this assignment as a conflict of interest when TSB was awarded the contract to abandon the well. It is not clear to this panel who he thought was making the decisions on the platform. The TSB

President did not coordinate the efforts of the various groups and personnel engaged in the project or see to it that his managers were effectively coordinating and consulting with one another.

TSB's Safety Manual's "Administrative Procedures" state in part "... that the President is invested with the ultimate responsibility for the safety and health protection of all Twachtman, Snyder & Byrd, Inc., employees and for the loss prevention of facilities and operations under his supervision."

The TSB Downhole Division Manager manages TSB's Downhole Division operations in Houma, Louisiana and reports to the TSB President. The TSB Downhole Division Manager is normally in charge of P&A wireline and e-line crews on the platform *(Attachment 9)* but was left out of the operations loop on this job *(Attachment 10)*. Although he did not understand the deceased's function on this job, he felt that the deceased had the authority to fire his crew, which is contrary to the testimony provided by the TSB President.

The TSB Downhole Division Manager further testified that there was nothing about this job that he considered "normal" as

- TSB does not do snubbing work, but he stated that TSB does not pull tubing on live wells during P&A operations;

- his crews are only experienced using casing jacks to pull casing on "dead wells" (wells not under pressure).

He initially selected personnel for this job to assist in e-line and wire line operations in support of a snubbing procedure that was to be conducted by another contractor (snubbing contractor). He did not know why the procedure changed from snubbing to casing jacks.

During the interviews, the TSB Downhole Division Manager stated that he would not have used the procedure that was proposed. He further stated that he would have incorporated the use of a snubbing unit for the job. Then, using a 1¼" work string, he would have tried either to pull the fish out of the well or push the fish out the bottom of the tubing. Only after exhausting this procedure would he have tried to lube and bleed in on the back side and strip out of the hole to a point below the fish for a hot tap.

22

The TSB Downhole Division Manager stated that he learned about the safety concerns of his crew when they returned early from the job and showed up at the office at 8 a.m. on Monday, February 20. He indicated that he probably would have shut down the job had he known about the unsafe working conditions on the platform. He subsequently rehired all but two crew members who left the job and were fired by the deceased.

The Day-crew and the Night-crew Supervisors

The day-crew and the night-crew supervisors supervised the crews on the platform and consulted with the deceased regarding the daily tasks. In addition to supervising the crews, they were responsible for

- writing the JSA's;

- holding a safety meeting at the beginning of each shift to review the JSA's for each task to be performed;

- maintaining a safe working environment by advising, monitoring, and enforcing the company safety rules and procedures in accordance with TSB's safety manual; and

- operating equipment as needed.

TSB's Safety Manual's "Statement of Management Safety and Environmental Policy" states in part:
Safety is line management responsibility. Supervisory staff at all levels are charged with the responsibility of ensuring that employees under their control, perform each job within the guidelines of all federal and state regulations as well as TSB and Client policy. Furthermore, strict compliance by all personnel to all federal and state regulations, as well as TSB and Client policy in the performance of their duties while on any TSB or Client work site is mandatory. Any employee not respecting these safety rules and government regulations will be subject to disciplinary action. Any unsafe acts or conditions must be reported to the supervisor, project manager, offshore manager and/or TSB management immediately. Ultimately, each employee is responsible for his own safety as well as the safety of those around him.

The supervisors normally reported to the TSB Downhole Division Manager, but on this job they were prohibited from doing so and only reported to the deceased. In general, the day crew conducted the lube and bleed operations (attempting to kill the well) while the night crew worked the casing jacks (attempting to free the stuck tubing). The day-crew supervisor testified that his crew also tested the BOP and that the deceased kept the test charts in his possession.

Neither supervisor had prior experience using casing jacks to P&A "live wells." The day-crew supervisor felt the use of casing jacks was "safe" but knew others disagreed and considered the procedure to be inappropriate and unsafe, given there was pressure on the well and that they were unable to kill the well successfully. The day-crew supervisor also felt he understood the pipe stripping procedure although he had never conducted an operation like this before. Others were critical of the procedure and feared that they could lose control of the well if the pipe rams failed.

The night-crew supervisor openly disagreed with both the deceased and the day-crew supervisor regarding job safety and felt the job was unsafe from the beginning. On his last shift prior to the accident, he was instructed by the deceased to pull and turn the pipe, which he refused to do. He felt that given the pressure on the annulus, they could not control the well if the pipe parted. He did not discuss his concerns with the TSB Downhole Division Manager or shut the job down. He wanted to get off the platform and indicated that he would have boarded the boat, along with the other men who left on December 19, if he had been awake at the time.

The TSB Consultant/FOC "Company Man" on the Platform ("The Deceased")
The deceased wore two hats on this job and had conflicting responsibilities as the onsite project manager for the primary contractor (TSB) and as FOC's "company man" on the platform *(see Attachments 8 & 10)*. He was employed with TSB's consulting group in Houston, Texas, as a P&A specialist/project manager and reported to the TSB President in charge of decommissioning and P&A operations. He was originally hired by the TSB Downhole Division Manager as a field supervisor for the downhole division before being transferred to the sales group (Houston) during or about May 2005. His assignments with the sales group included the preparation of estimates, proposals, and procedures for downhole operations. He was hired by FOC's Office Consultant in December 2005 as TSB's P&A consultant and FOC's "company man" on the platform for the B-11 well abandonment. According to the TSB President, the deceased was being paid by TSB and, to the TSB President's knowledge, was not being paid by FOC.

24

According to FOC personnel interviewed, FOC was not paying the deceased directly but were paying TSB.

According to interview statements, the FOC Operations Manager did not know of the deceased's affiliation with TSB prior to the accident and would have been uncomfortable with that arrangement (because of the conflicting roles and divided loyalties) if he had known. The TSB President did not consider the deceased to be FOC's "company man" on the platform, although he did consider him to be working for FOC and to be TSB's primary contact with FOC and conversely. In his opinion, the deceased was on the platform to coordinate the crews and to consult with the TSB Downhole Division Manager on operational matters. According to the TSB president, the deceased was responsible (on this project) for the

- coordination and continuity of two downhole division crews (TSB's field supervisors reported to the deceased instead of the TSB Downhole Division Manager throughout the operation (*see Attachment 10*);

- coordination of equipment and materials; and

- transfer of information, including daily reports, between FOC and TSB.

According to the TSB President, the deceased did not have the authority to fire downhole division personnel; however, this viewpoint is not shared by the TSB Downhole Division Manager.

During the preparation phase, the deceased conducted several site visits to the platform to assess conditions and subsequently recommended substituting casing jacks for snubbing equipment. After TSB was awarded the contract to P&A the well, the deceased told the TSB Downhole Division Manager that "me and FOC are running this job; it's not your concern." The TSB Downhole Division Manager provided the equipment and personnel. After the job was mobilized and the vessel left the dock for the job site (on or about February 13, 2006), the deceased had no further verbal communications with either the TSB President or the TSB Downhole Division Manager.

Between February 13 and 20, 2006, according to TSB crewmembers interviewed, the deceased

- Fired personnel for refusing to stay on the facility while the boat left the field;

- Made operational decisions without consulting with anyone offsite;

- Acted "differently" on this job ("taking risks") according to some observers, while others considered his behavior to be "normal" for him ("safe");

- Disregarded comments and complaints from various personnel regarding long hours, inadequate housing, cold food, unsafe working conditions/work practices, poor housekeeping practices, and equipment problems;

- Communicated daily with FOC and TSB managers via email (morning reports) and with FOC's office consultant via telephone/cell phone in the morning and as needed during the day;

- Criticized the crew for making telephones calls to the office and prohibited further telephone communication between platform personnel and management, particularly with the TSB Downhole Division Manager;

- Worked the casing jacks without FOC's knowledge or consent;

- Operated the annular preventer (Hydril) in reverse ("open" was closed and "closed" was open) to save time in lieu of correcting the problem;

- By-passed safety systems and created pollution (opened the Hydril and conducted the lube and bleed procedure through the choke and kill lines instead of through the gas buster; vented well fluids and gases into the atmosphere/water, causing pollution), and

- Pulled the pipe on the morning of February 20, causing the pipe to part.

Conclusions

Causes

It is the conclusion of this panel that, on the morning of February 20, 2006, the deceased attempted to free the stuck tubing string on the B-11 well. In doing so, he exceeded the yield strength of the tubing when he pulled approximately 135,000 pounds on the tubing, causing it to part. This action resulted in the tubing and slips being ejected from the wellbore, the slips fatally striking the deceased as he attempted to evacuate the area, and a brief loss of well control. It is also the conclusion of this panel that the deceased did not calculate enough of a safety factor when he determined maximum amount pull for the grade of pipe.

Contributing Causes

Prudent operations plans would have been to shut this operation down on the 17th, when TSB could not contain wellbore pressure, and use more appropriate equipment such as a snubbing unit. A snubbing unit is designed to perform downhole operations and can remove tubing while keeping the wellbore pressure under control. The fish in the tubing magnified their problem, and they were using basically seawater to control the flow when a higher density fluid was needed. The method they were using to plug and abandon the well – using casing jacks – should only be used if a well is dead and there is virtually no chance of any pressure being on the wellbore.

The operation should have been shut down. The procedure should then have been revised to use appropriate equipment for the circumstances and submitted to MMS for approval before continuing further. This decisionmaking process was complicated, since the person in charge represented both FOC and TSB.

The deceased made operational decisions on the platform without consulting either FOC's or TSB's offsite managers. His decisions and actions placed the platform, personnel, and environment in constant threat from a potential loss of well control, and resulted in a brief loss of well control, pollution, and a fatal accident. The two TSB field supervisors had differing opinions about the conduct and safety of the operation. Neither supervisor shut down the job in spite of the safety violations, unsafe work practices, and attendant pollution. Further, neither man attempted to report what was happening on the platform to the TSB Downhole Division Manager.

Therefore, this panel concludes that the lack of appropriate equipment (snubbing unit) and appropriately trained personnel are contributing causes to this incident. Additionally, poor judgment and decisionmaking by the deceased and TSB's field supervisors on the platform are also considered contributing causes to this incident

Possible Contributing Causes

Offsite Management Failures

    FOC's Operations Manager

FOC's Operations Manager for the Gulf Coast Region approved the equipment substitution but didn't revise the actual procedures or require that they be revised. He felt the operation was safe given certain assumptions that he didn't attempt to verify. He was kept informed of the progress by the FOC office consultant, but was generally disengaged from the day-to-day operation and on personal time during the long holiday weekend when the accident occurred. He left the day-to-day conduct and oversight of the operation to offsite and onsite consultants, but didn't inquire about the deceased's background and affiliations. Although he indicated that he would have shut down the operation had he known the details about the deceased's lube and bleed procedure and the resulting pollution, he failed to follow up after he requested a copy of the procedure and didn't receive one.

As FOC's Operations Manager for the platform, he was detached from the day-to-day operations and did not

- Effectively manage the project,

- Ensure that the operation was conducted in a safe and workmanlike manner,

- Ensure that personnel and the environment were protected, and

- Ensure that pollution would be prevented.

28

FOC's Office Consultant

FOC's Office Consultant in charge of the operation was uninformed about the serious equipment problems, poor housekeeping conditions, unsafe work practices, and pollution resulting from operations on the platform. After a site visit in December 2005, he never visited the platform again until after the accident. Although he was misinformed about the day-to-day progress and conduct of the operation by the deceased, he never personally inspected the operation despite the recurring difficulties encountered killing the well, as verified in the morning reports. He specifically failed to

- Recognize the potential conflict of interest created by allowing the deceased to represent simultaneously both FOC's interests and TSB's interests on the job;

- Effectively oversee the conduct of the operation;

- Ensure that the operation was conducted in a safe and workmanlike manner;

- Ensure the protection of personnel and the environment;

- Ensure the prevention of pollution; and

- Ensure and verify that all required tests of the blow out prevention equipment were conducted and documented.

TSB's President

TSB's President considered this to be an unusual job for TSB; however, he was completely disengaged from the day-to-day management and oversight of the operation and did not communicate directly with the deceased after approving his assignment. He was unaware of the internal and external communications problems within the organization, the lack of a clear chain of command structure for this project, the operational problems and safety issues on the platform, and the generic ("canned") JSA's. He assumed his personnel were coordinating and communicating effectively with one another.

TSB's president apparently never had a clear understanding of FOC's intention to use the deceased as their "company man" on the platform or envisioned this assignment as a conflict of interest when TSB

29

was awarded the contract to abandon the well. It is not clear to the panel members who he thought was making the decisions on the platform. TSB's President did not coordinate the efforts of the various groups and personnel engaged in the project or see to it that his managers were effectively coordinating and consulting with one another.

Considering the new and unusual roles, responsibilities, and tasks assigned to the separate groups and personnel assigned to the project, TSB's President failed to

- Manage, coordinate, and integrate the tasks of project personnel;

- Recognize the potential conflict of interest created by allowing the deceased to represent simultaneously both FOC's interests and TSB's interests on the job;

- Establish clear lines of authority, responsibility, and communication between key personnel on the project; and

- Ensure that everyone connected with the project understood their jobs and were effectively coordinating and communicating with one another.

TSB's Downhole Division Manager

TSB's Downhole Division Manager was intentionally left out of the operations and communications structure throughout much of the operation by the deceased. He became concerned when he learned that some of his crew had been fired for leaving the job early and had indicated they left for a variety of safety-related and other reasons. He attempted unsuccessfully to reach the platform by telephone but did not attempt to visit the platform. He disagreed with the revised equipment and procedural changes and did not understand why the deceased was managing the project, but apparently did not communicate his concerns to TSB's President. His view of his role and responsibilities on this project was significantly different from the TSB President's views. TSB's Downhole Division Manager was not personally responsible for writing the JSA's for tasks performed by his crews. That task apparently fell to the supervisors in the field. However, all the JSA's we reviewed for a given task looked generic ("canned"), regardless of the date or time the task was performed, and didn't appear to have been reviewed or revised by anyone associated with this project to reflect the unique tasks and safety considerations of the job.

As the individual normally in charge of field personnel conducting P&A operations, TSB's Downhole Division Manager was not consulted with or kept abreast of the conduct and progress of the operation, except through e-mail transmissions of the morning reports from the platform. We do not know if he questioned or attempted to remedy the situation. Beyond the communications problems on the platform, which were out of his control, he failed to

- Clarify his role and responsibilities on the project with upper management,

- Coordinate effectively with the other key personnel involved in the project,

- Communicate with downhole division personnel (field supervisors and crews) on the platform, and

- Review and recommend revisions to JSA's to reflect the unique tasks and safety considerations on the job.

Onsite Management Failures
  FOC's "Company Man" on the Platform (The Deceased)
The deceased generally kept his own counsel and made operational decisions on his own or in consultation with the TSB day-crew supervisor. The panel members received contradictory and perplexing testimony of the deceased's demeanor and attitude on this job. According to some, he acted "normally," while others viewed his demeanor as "different" on this job. Many crewmembers and one supervisor were concerned about safety and felt the job was unsafe and should be shut down. Prior to the accident, one injured crew member and five others left the job early for various reasons, leaving the tower crews on the platform shorthanded. Daytime and nighttime operations continued in spite of the manpower shortages and in opposition to the manpower requirements as described in the JSA's. The deceased's decisions and actions engendered that opinion and fostered an atmosphere of tension and fear among the

crewmembers who left the job on February 19, as well as many of those who remained on the platform. The panel members have been unable to identify a motive for the deceased's apparent "different" behavior on this job. The panel members can only conclude that many of the unsafe and unworkmanlike practices, equipment failures, safety violations, and incidents on the platform are directly and indirectly related to decisions made and actions taken by the deceased.

In the panel members' opinion, the deceased made a number of inappropriate decisions and actions that negatively affected the operation. As FOC's representative (and TSB's project coordinator) on the platform, the deceased exceeded his authorities and failed to

- Communicate verbally with anyone offsite at TSB and was openly critical of communication between the crew and TSB's offsite management and prohibited further communications, particularly with the TSB Downhole Division Manager;

- Provide FOC's managers with complete and accurate information regarding the conduct, problems, and progress of the operation (i.e., safety-related issues, unsafe work practices, poor housekeeping, equipment problems, pollution, etc.);

- Conduct the operation in a safe, workmanlike, and environmentally sound manner (i.e., exposed the facility, personnel, and environment to unsafe conditions, loss of well control, pollution, and serious injury);

- Consult with TSB's Downhole Division Manager and TSB crew supervisors to review and revise the JSA's to address the unique procedures and safety considerations on the job (e.g., use of casing jacks to pull pipe and P&A a well under pressure);

- Test and operate the blowout prevention equipment as required and intended;

- Prevent pollution;

- Maintain a "wall" between himself and the TSB crew, and "take no chances" per FOC's instruction;

- Shut down 24-hour operations because of manpower shortages; and

- Address safety concerns raised by personnel (i.e., job safety, the use of casing jacks, pulling pipe under excessive tension, lube and bleed procedures, shut down job, etc.).

TSB's Day-Crew and Night-Crew Supervisors

The TSB day and night crew supervisors on the platform were specifically responsible for writing JSA's on the job to reflect every aspect of the job. Although they disagreed about the safety of the operation, both supervisors failed to

- Inform the TSB Downhole Division Manager of the unsafe and unworkmanlike procedures and conditions or the safety concerns of the crew;

- Shut down the job because of unsafe work practices, lack of personnel, or to prevent pollution;

- Require workers to wear proper safety equipment, as indicated in TSB's safety manual (fall protection gear);

- Revise the JSA's to reflect changes in the tasks performed or the equipment used on the job, or to reflect safety concerns related to plugging and abandoning a "live well" by using casing jacks; and

- Conduct effective safety meetings with the crews.

On the basis of this information, it is concluded by the panel members that ineffective management and supervision of the operation by both FOC and TSB (at all levels) is a possible contributing cause of this incident. Upper management at FOC and TSB were detached from the field operation and failed to provide direct oversight and control. At TSB, no effective chain of command structure was in place and no one in the office was overseeing the operation. FOC relied entirely on consultants to supervise the operation onsite and offsite.

Recommendations

Safety Alert

This investigative panel recommends that the MMS should issue a Safety Alert to industry regarding this incident. The Safety Alert should briefly describe the accident and identify all the causes. The following recommendations should be made to industry:

- When conducting this type of operation, operators should maintain adequate oversight of the contractors by whatever means to ensure that the contractor is not taking any unnecessary shortcuts and that the contractor is following industry-accepted practices.

- Operators should conduct a pre-job meeting with **all** involved parties. The purpose of the meeting should be to outline the scope of work to be conducted and the manpower requirements, identify lines of authority and responsibility, outline the process for managing changes in the job, and stress the importance of "Stop Work" authority and reporting unsafe acts and conditions.

- When using consultants as the operator representative, operators should require a site inspection by an operator representative employed by the operator prior to the commencement of work to verify that the equipment is rigged up according to approved plans and methods.

- Operators should require the contractors to provide detailed activity logs of the work being performed.

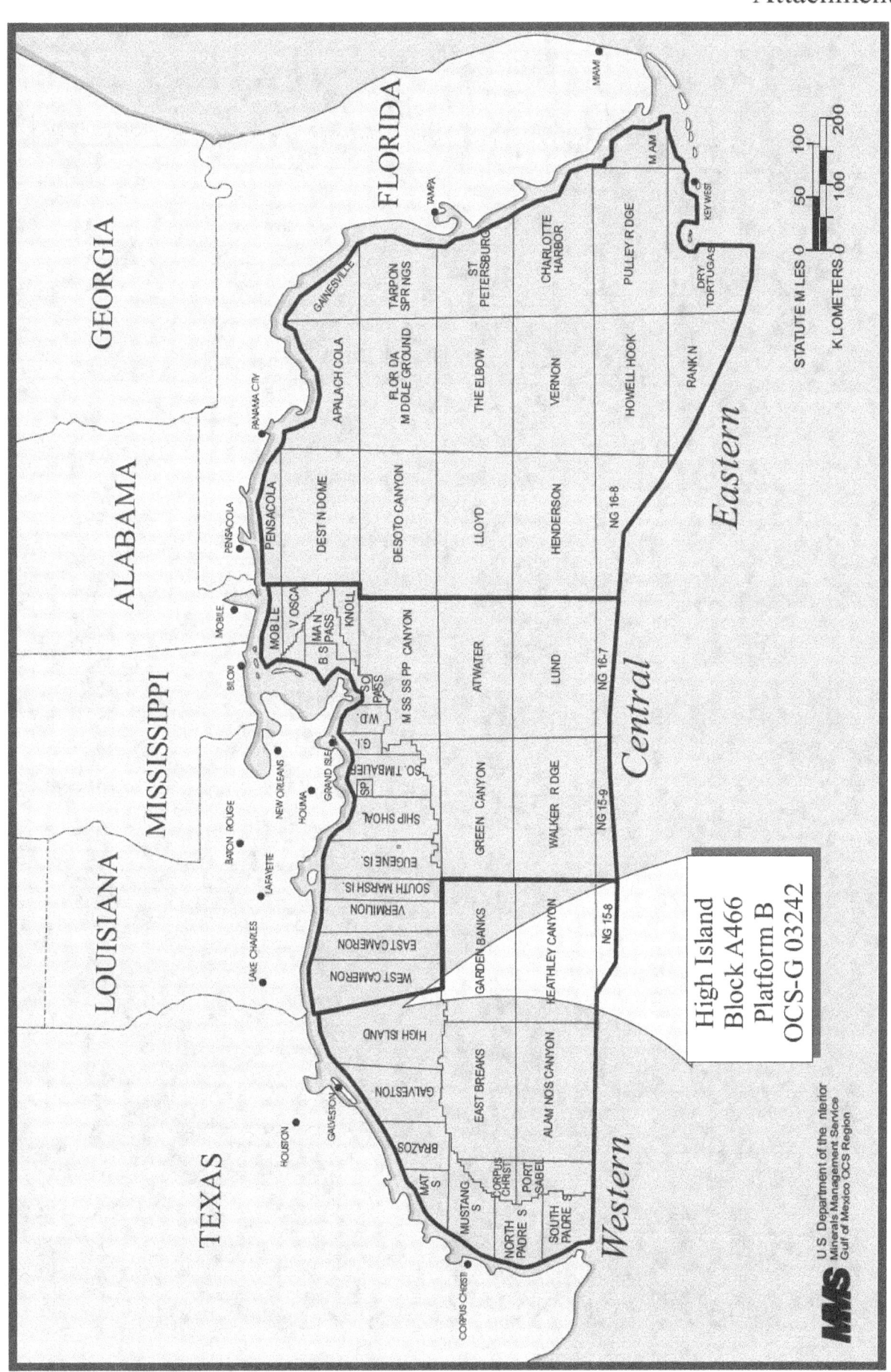

Location of Lease OCS-G 03242, High Island Block A466, Platform B.

Photograph of High Island Block A466 Platform "B"

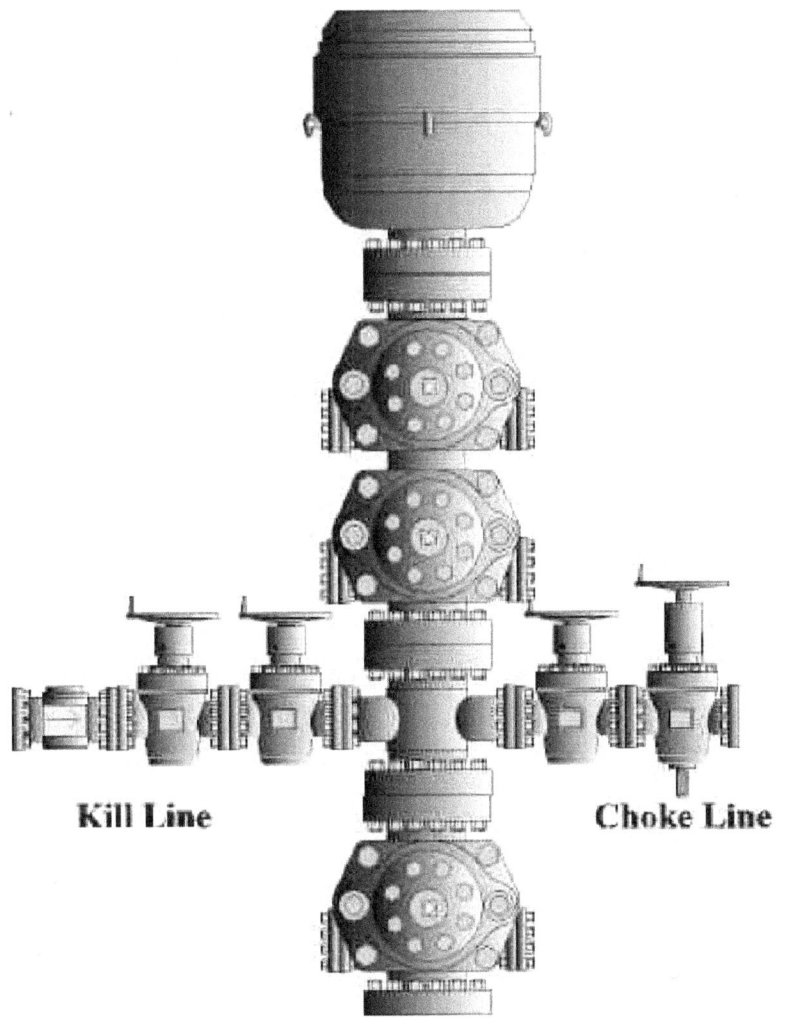

Annular BOP

Pipe Ram

Blind Ram

Kill Line   Choke Line

Flow Cross

Pipe Ram

Diagram of Approved BOP Configuration

Photograph of BOP Stack on Location

Photograph of TSB Crewmember Working Without Fall Protection

Photograph of Bleeding Gas at BOP Stack

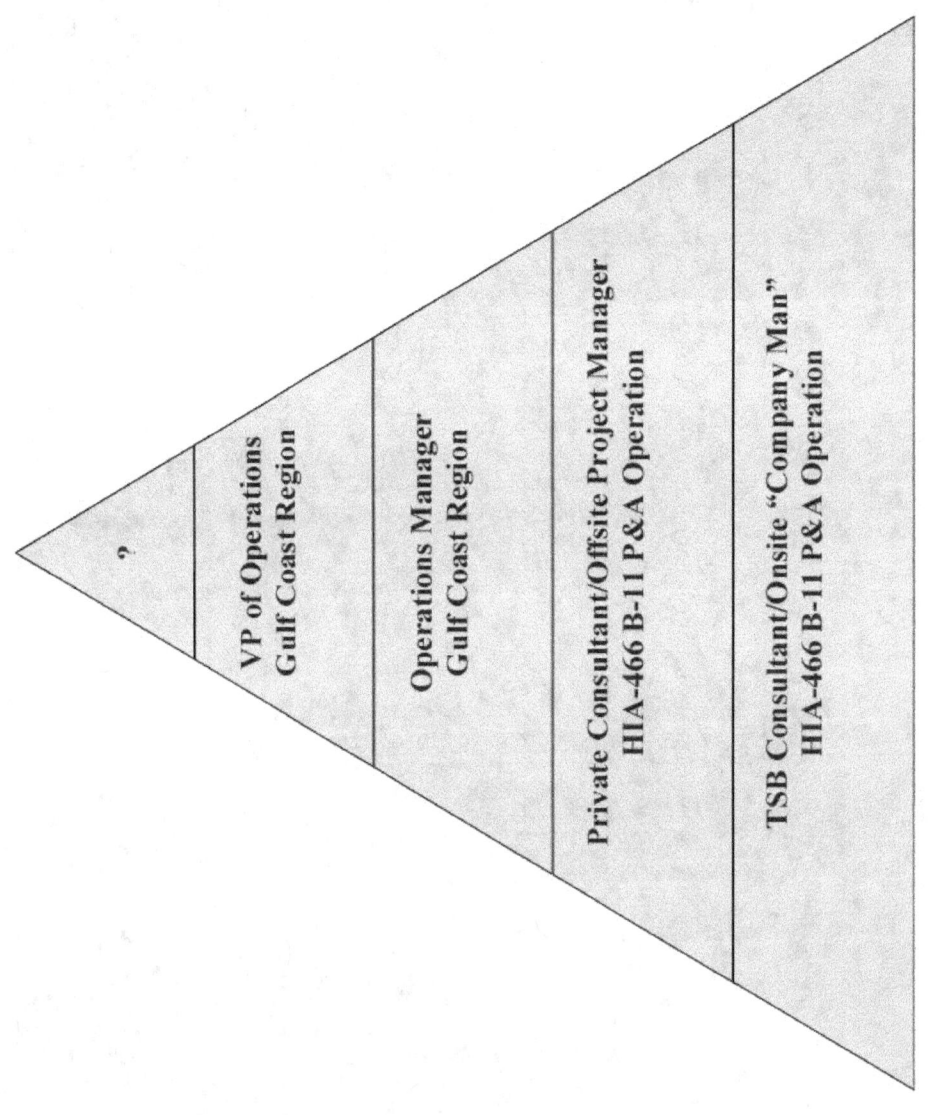

?

**VP of Operations
Gulf Coast Region**

**Operations Manager
Gulf Coast Region**

**Private Consultant/Offsite Project Manager
HIA-466 B-11 P&A Operation**

**TSB Consultant/Onsite "Company Man"
HIA-466 B-11 P&A Operation**

Forest Oil Company Chain of Command (At time of Incident)

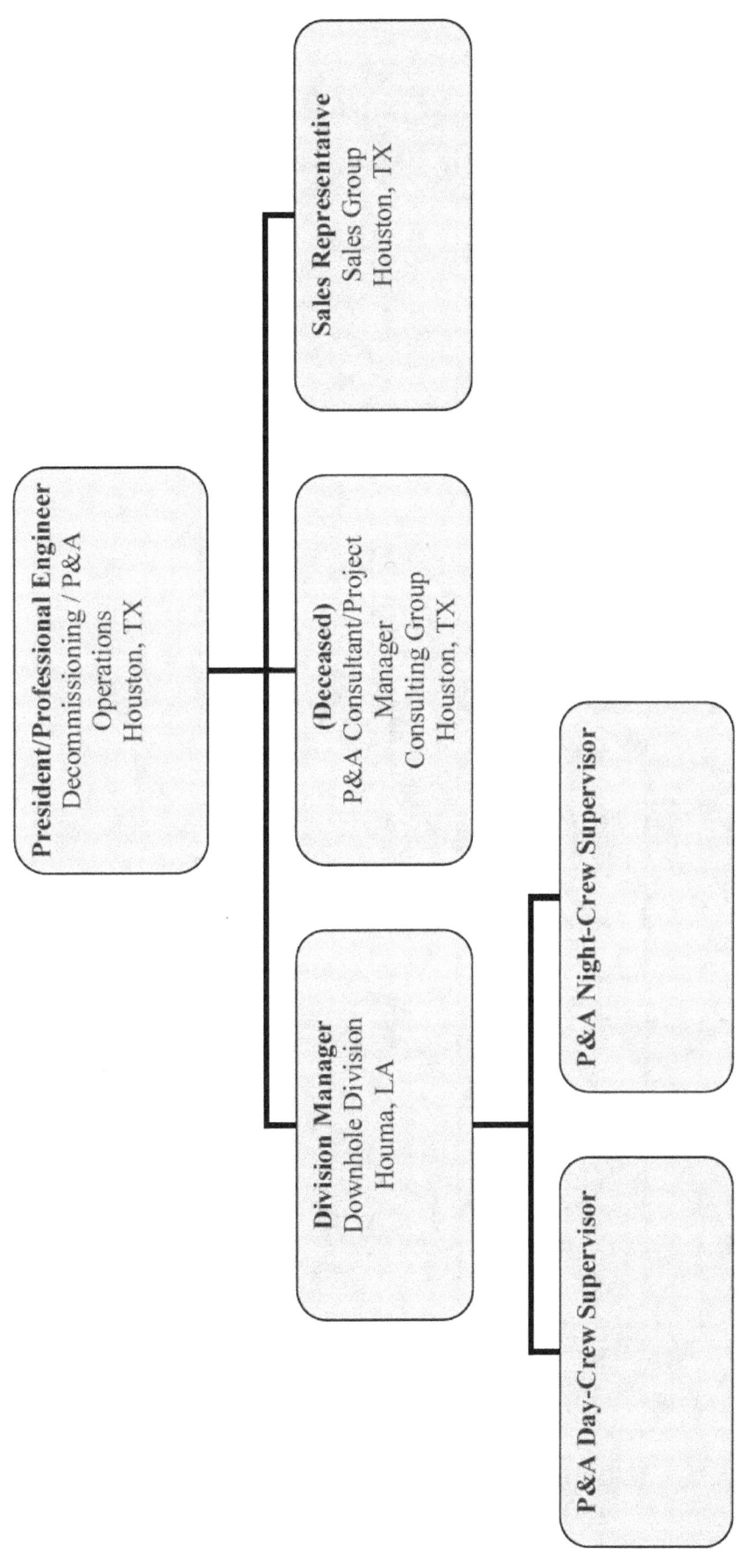

Twachtman, Snyder & Byrd Inc., Chain of Command (Normal P&A Operation)

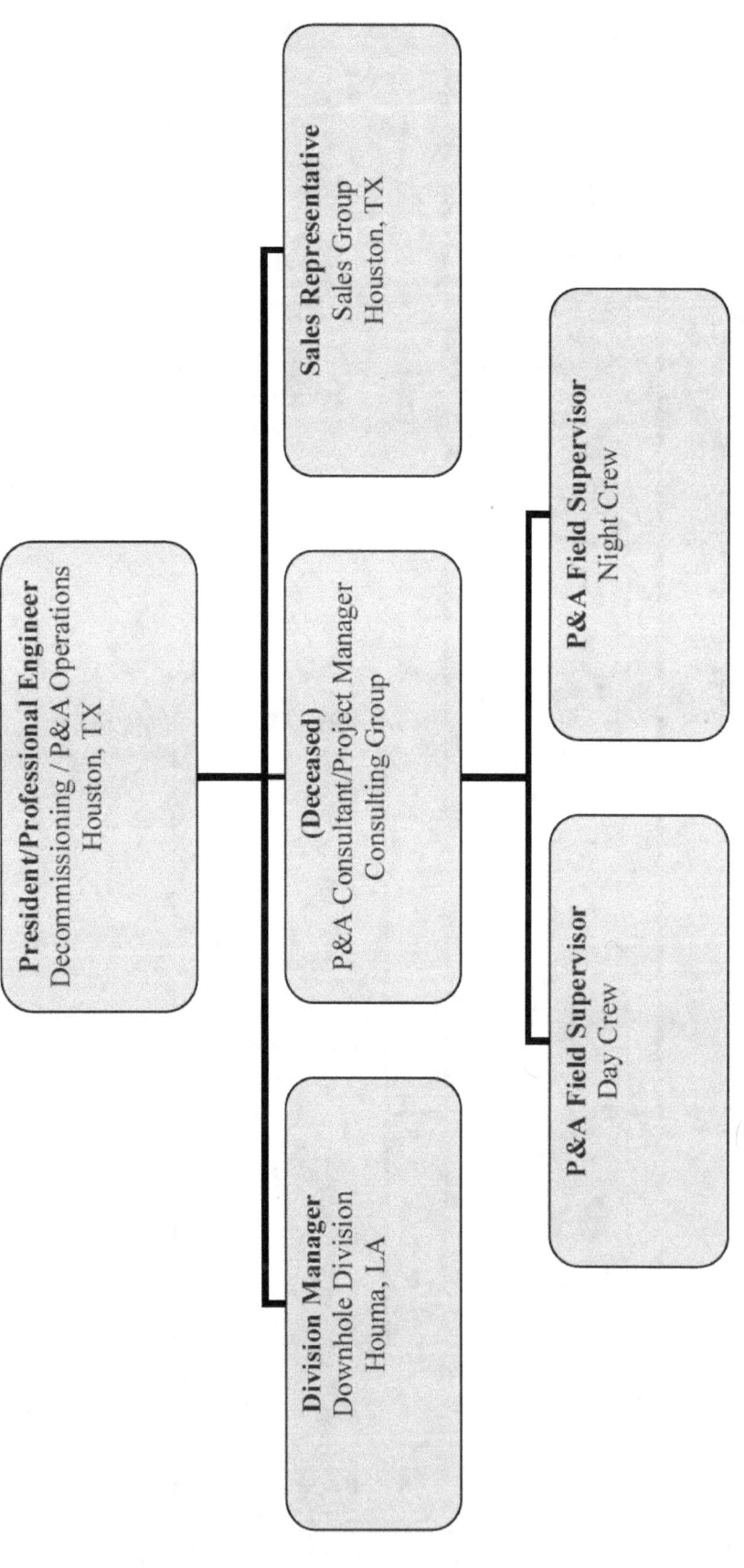

Twachtman, Snyder & Byrd Inc., Chain of Command (HI' A466 P&A Operations)